Back to Basics

ENGLISH

for 5-6 year olds

BOOK TWO

Sheila Lane and Marion Kemp

Aa Bb Cc Dd

Big A

little a

bouncing B

the Cat's in the cupboard and can't see D

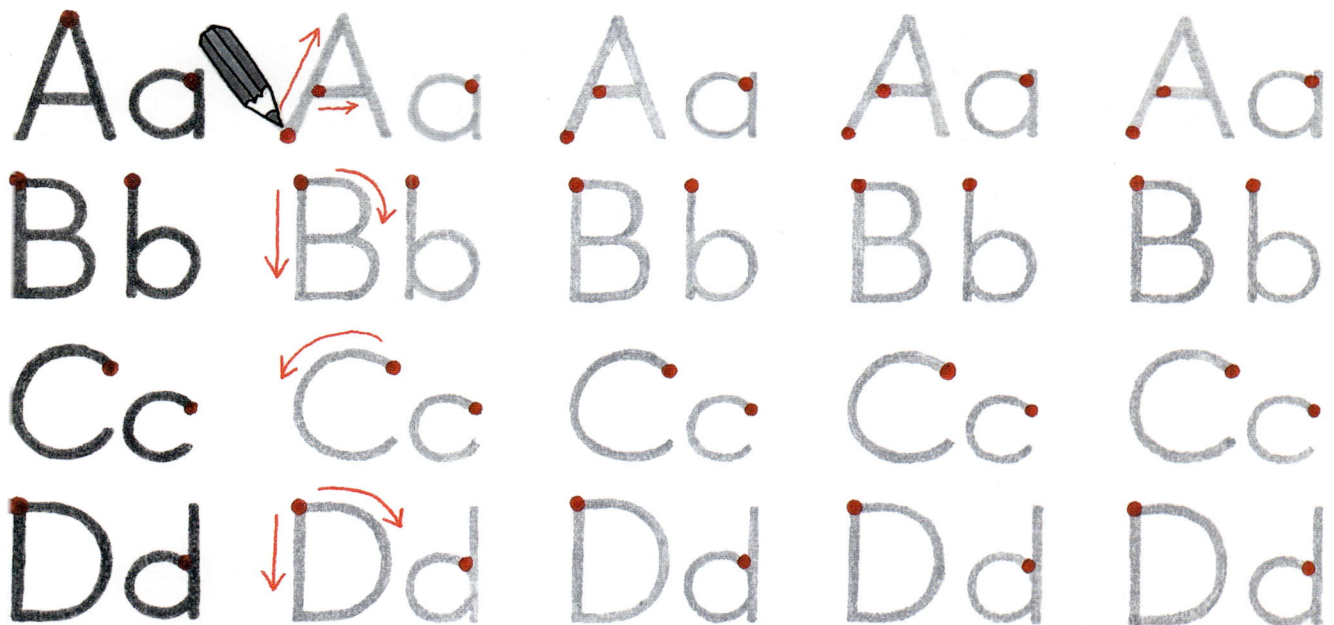

Write the missing letters.

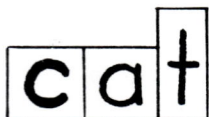

Write **a** or **c**.

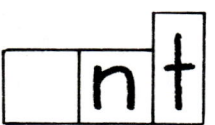

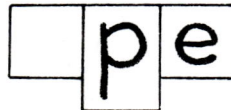

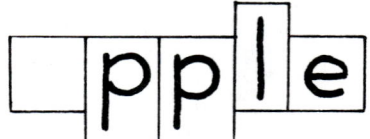

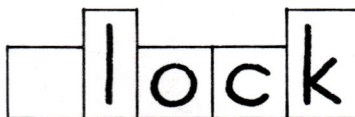

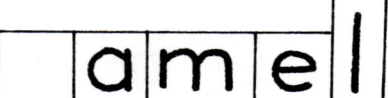

dog

butterfly

Write **b** or **d**.

☐ all

☐ us

☐ uck

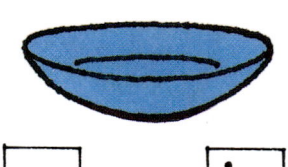
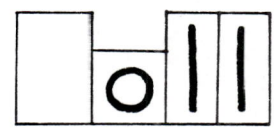

☐ oll

☐ at

☐ ish

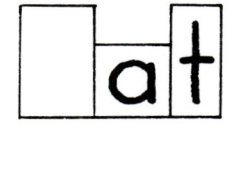
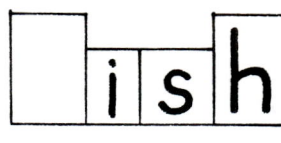

☐ anana

☐ inosaur

sun

Match the words and pictures.

a sun
a rainbow
a moon

a rainbow
a moon
a star

a moon
a rainbow
a sun

a sun
a moon
a rainbow

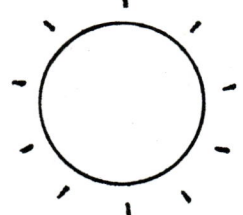

bus car lorry van boat

Draw a ring round yes or no.

Is it a van?  (yes) / no

Is it a boat?  yes / (no)

Is it a lorry?  yes / no

Is it a car?  yes / no

Is it a bus? 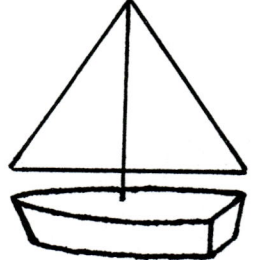 yes / no

Ee Ff Gg Hh

Match the capital letter with the small letter.

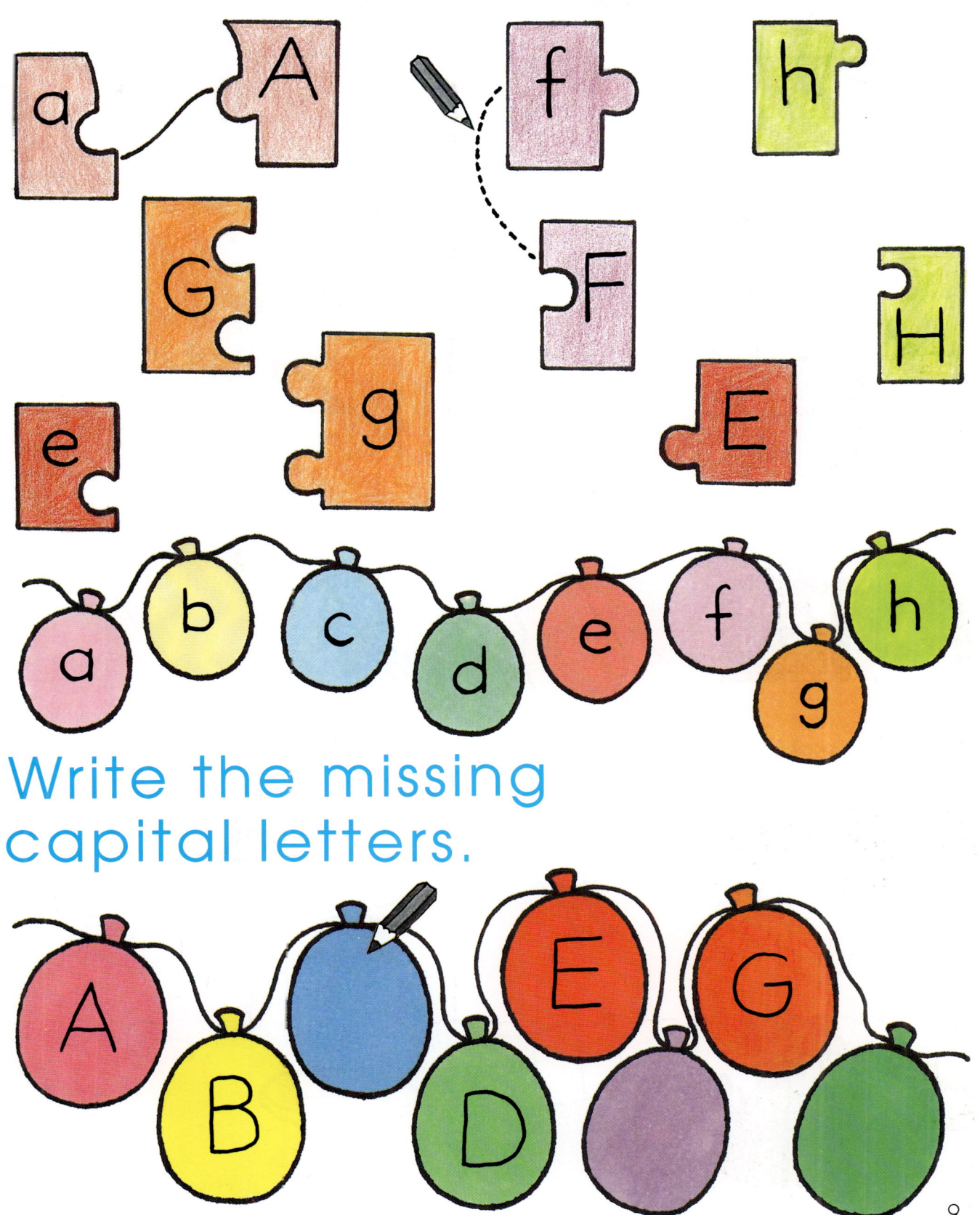

Write the missing capital letters.

  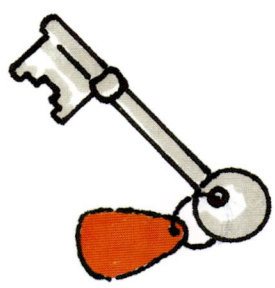  

Match the sounds and pictures.

   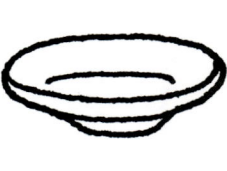 

(c) or s

Draw a ring round the right letter.

c or s    m or n   w or y

b or d   z or x   j or g

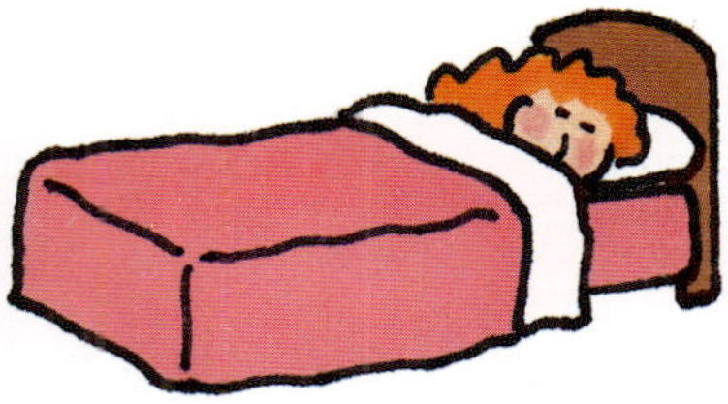

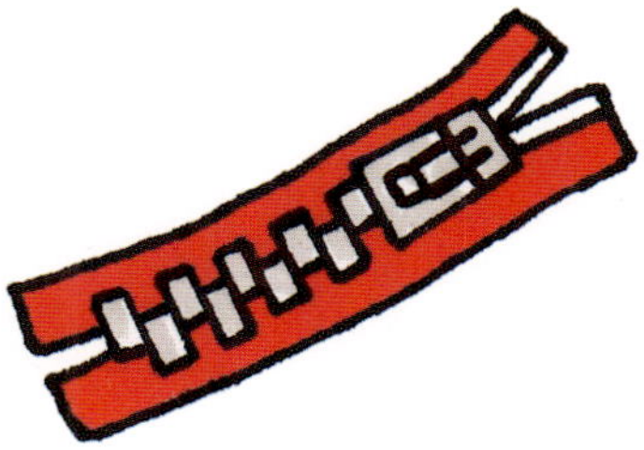

u or v   l or f   p or b

r or t   q or p   h or n

Look at me!

I can hop.

Write over the sentences.

I can run.

I can jump.

I can read.

I can write.

I can write my name.

Can a pig run?
yes

Write **yes** or **no**.

Can a dog read?

Can a frog hop?

Can a cat write?

Can a horse jump?

Ii Jj Kk Ll Mm Nn

Mm Mm Mm Mm

Nn Nn Nn Nn

Join the letters to make a star.

a

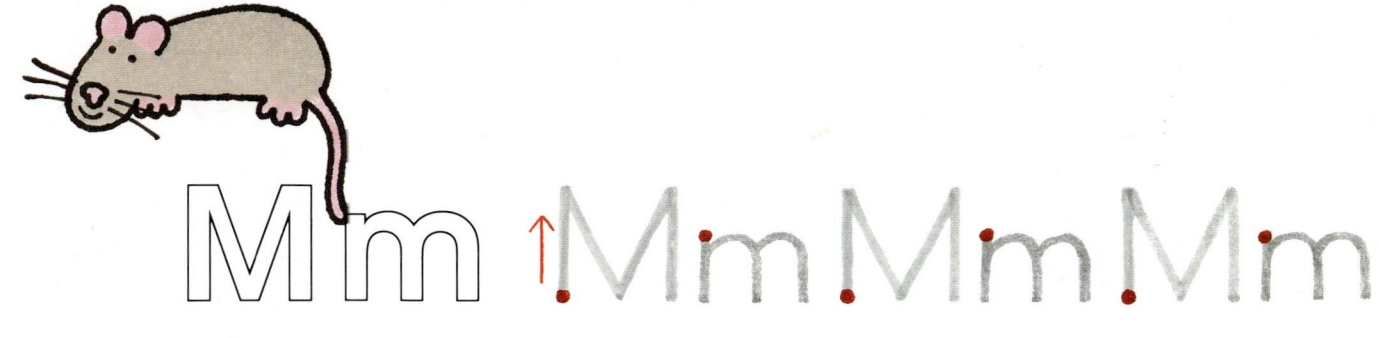

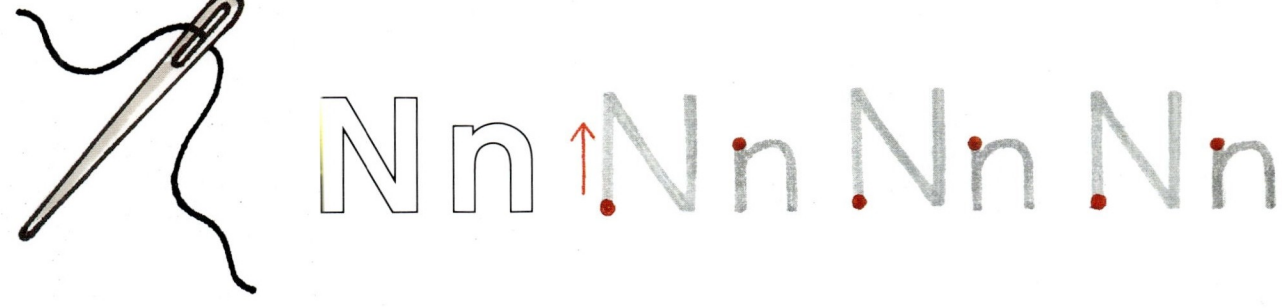

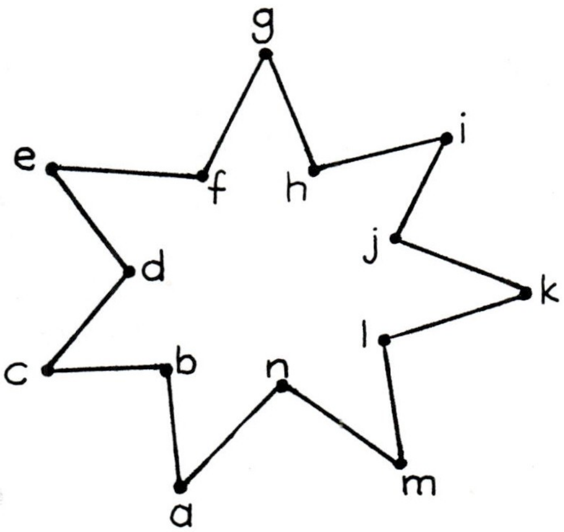

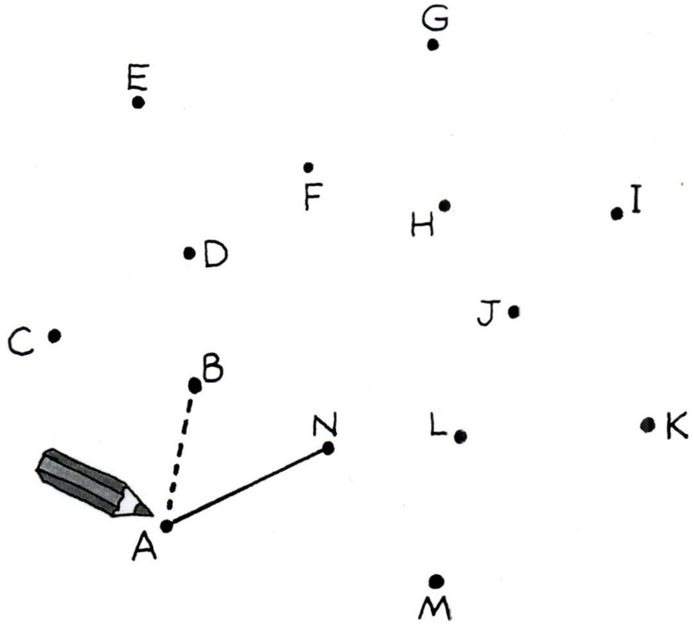

bun　egg　pear

fish　sweet　cake

Draw a ring round the right word.

I can eat ...

sun
(bun)

leg
egg

cake
rake

sweet
feet

dish
fish

pear
bear

Can you eat it?      Yes, I can.

      No, I cannot.

Yes, I can.      No, I cannot.

Write the sentence.

Y____ , ____ .   ____ , ____ .

____ , ____ .   ____ , ____ .

 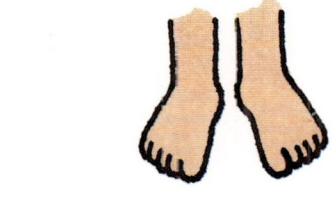

____ , ____ .   ____ , ____ .

____ , ____ .   ____ , ____ .

c for cup a for apple t for tree

c a t "That's me!"

Write the sounds in the boxes.

d for drum ☐ for owl ☐ for gate

☐ ☐ ☐ "That's me!"

☐ for hand ☐ for egg ☐ for net

☐ ☐ ☐ "That's me!"

☐ for moon ☐ for apple ☐ for nest

☐ ☐ ☐ "That's me!"

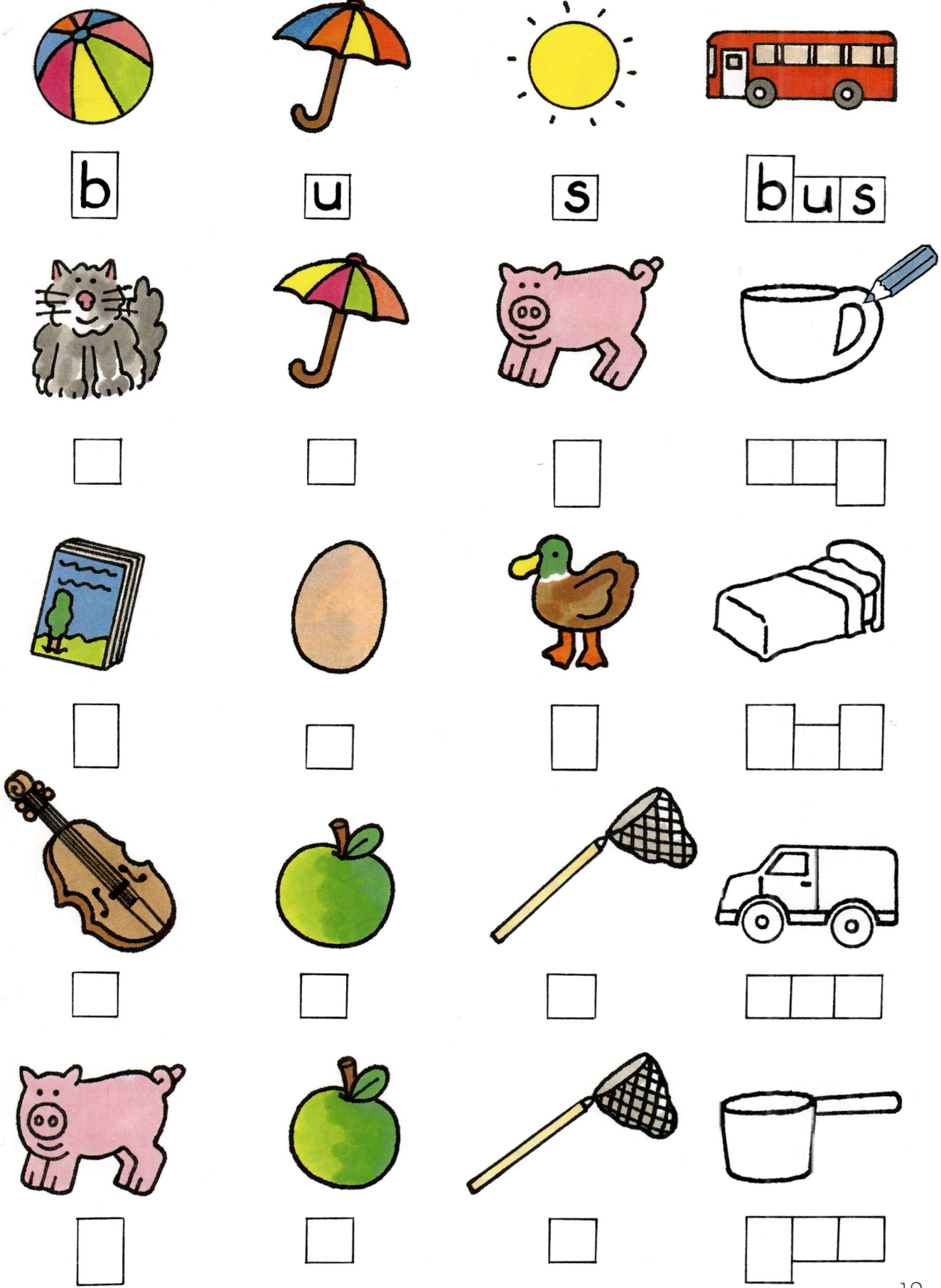

Write your name...

...on the book   ...on the picture

...in the card   ...in the book

Little Jack Horner sat in a corner.

Colour in and write over the names.

Lucy Locket lost her pocket

Simple Simon met a pieman.

Jack and Jill went up the hill.

Little Miss Muffet sat on a tuffet.

Write the sounds.

h

a

t

hat

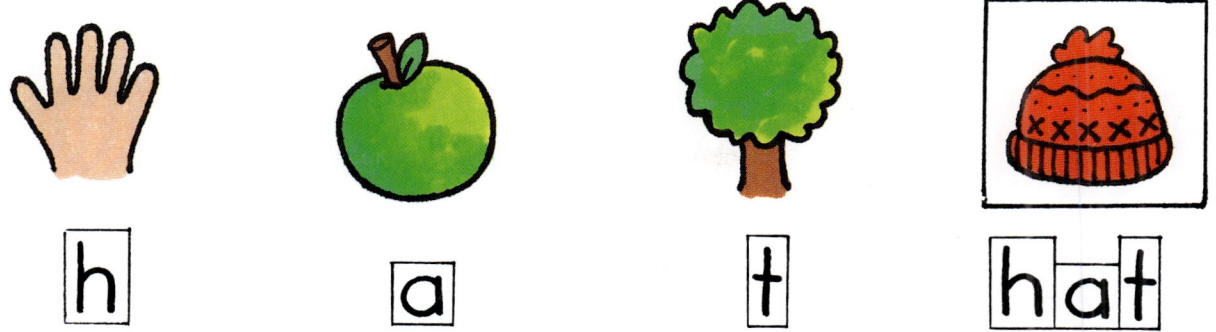

Write the sounds and draw the pictures.

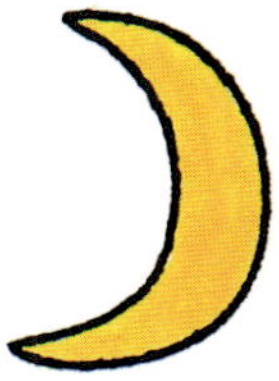

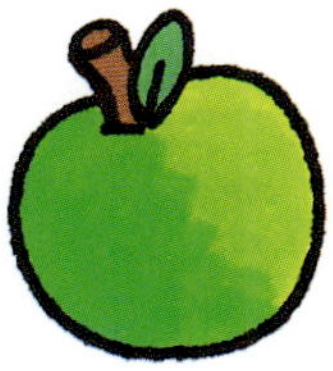

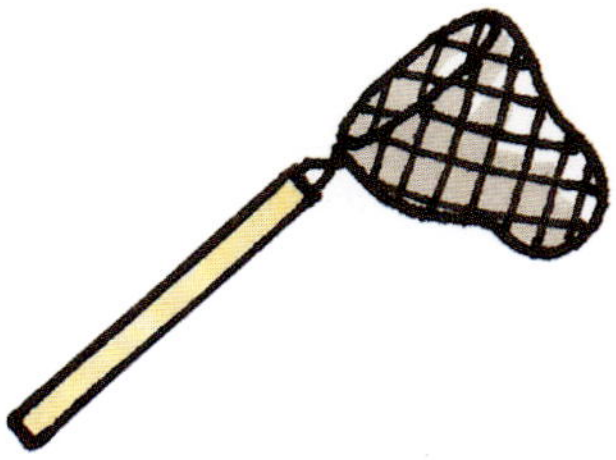

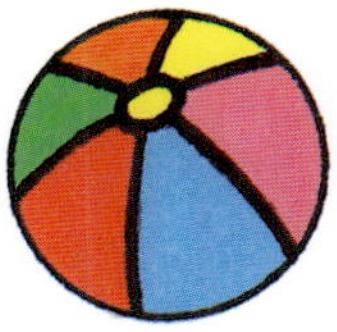

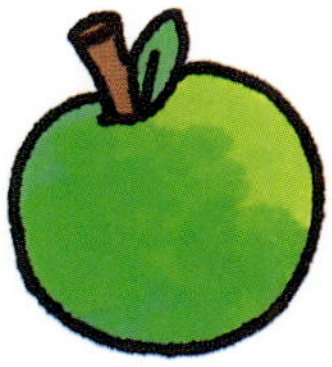

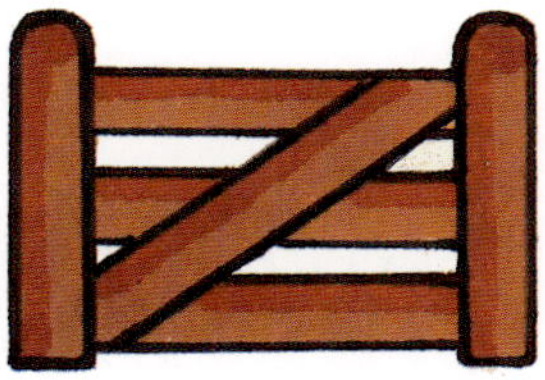

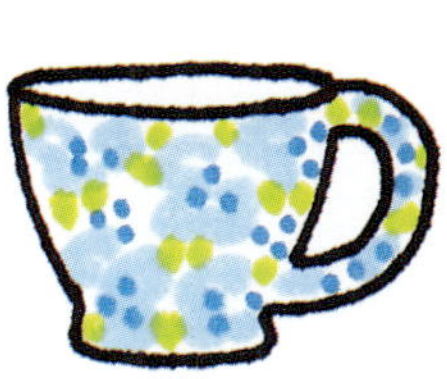

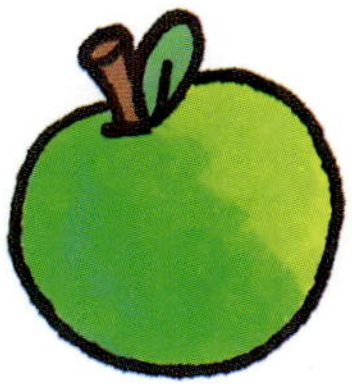

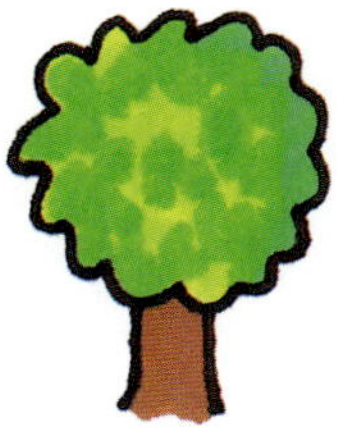

Uu Vv Ww Xx Yy Zz

Uu Uu Uu Uu Uu

Vv Vv Vv Vv Vv

Ww Ww Ww Ww

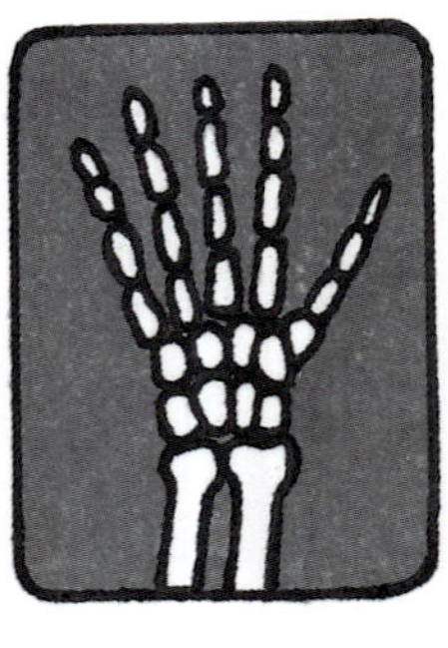

Xx Xx Xx Xx Xx

Yy Yy Yy Yy Yy

Zz Zz Zz Zz Zz

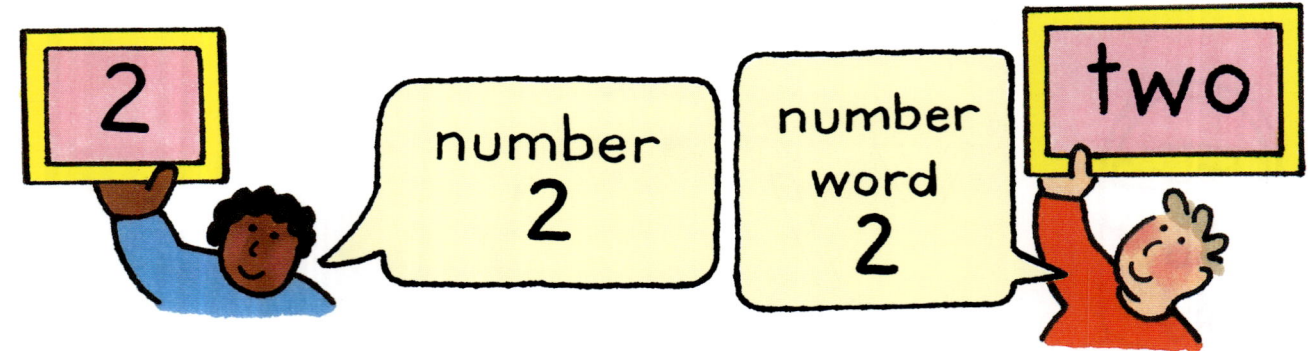

Write over the number words.

1 one
2 two
3 three
4 four
5 five
6 six
7 seven
8 eight
9 nine
10 ten

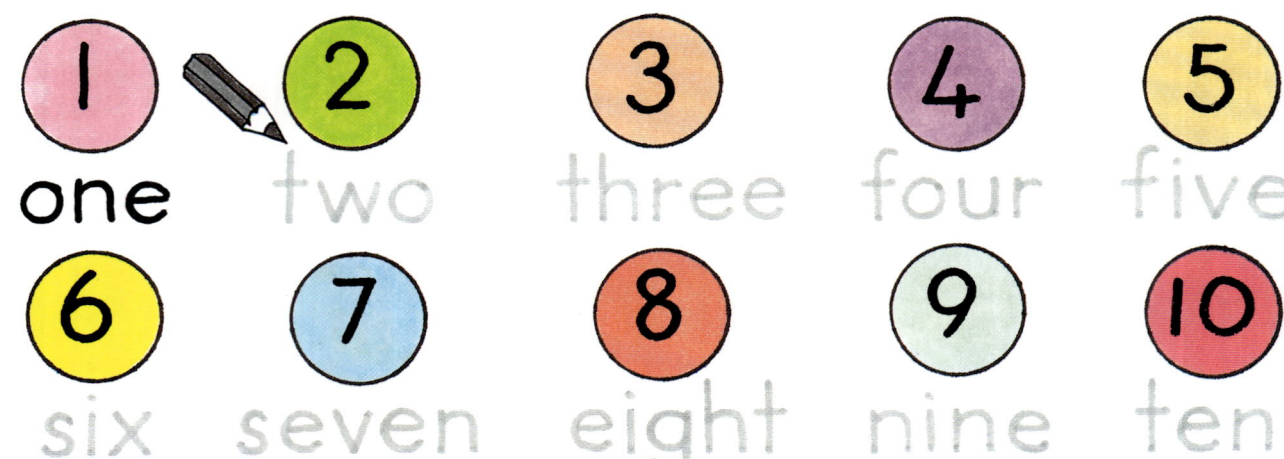

Write the number words.

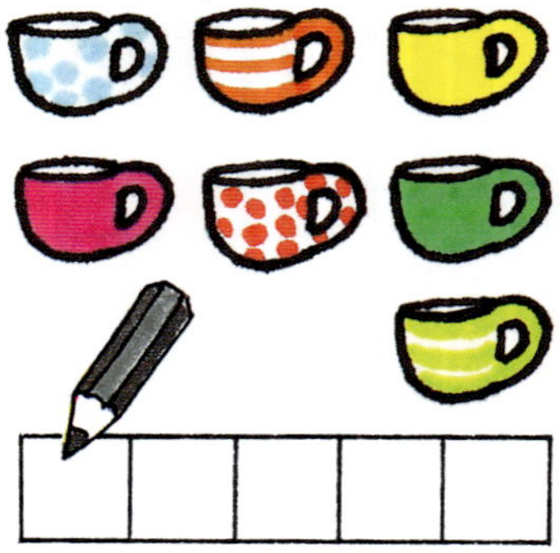

cups

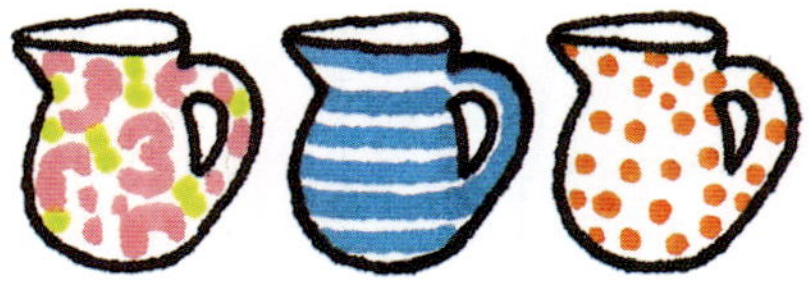

jugs

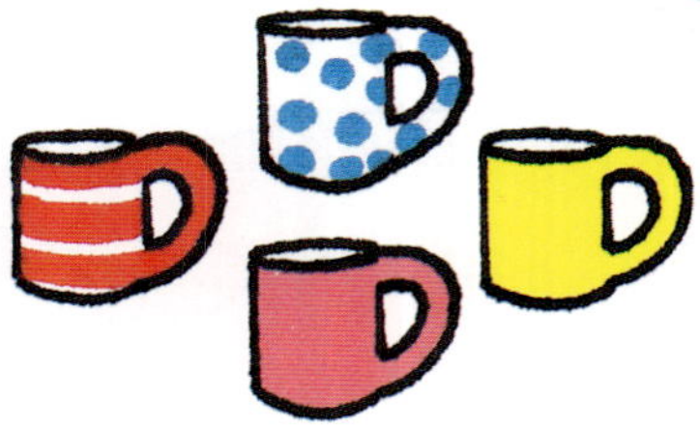

mugs

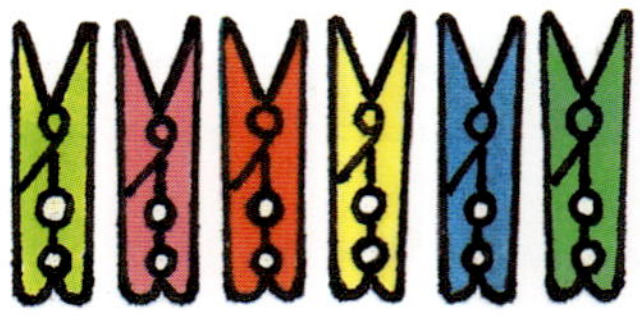

pegs

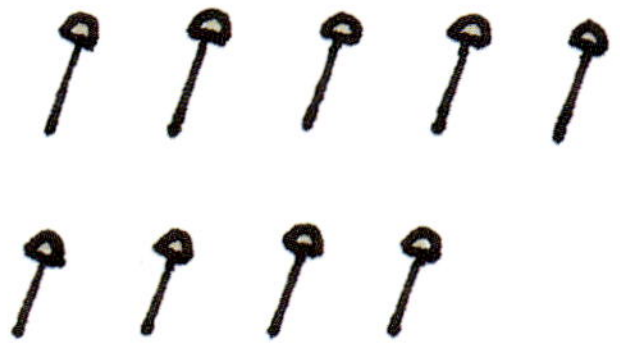

pins

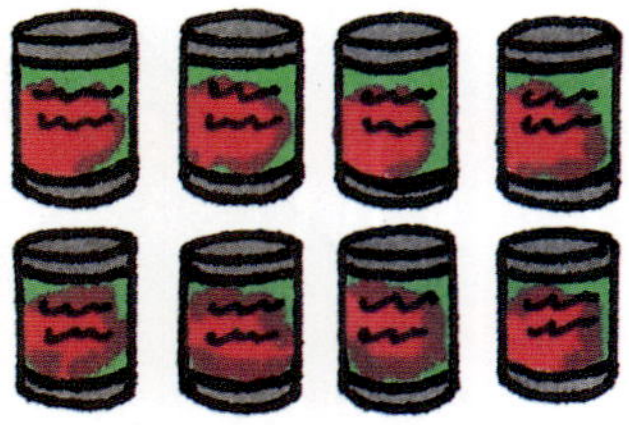

tins

Write the number words.

1 one   2 _ _ _

3 _ _ _ _ _   4 _ _ _ _ _   5 _ _ _ _

Once I caught a fish alive,

6 _ _ _ _   7 _ _ _ _ _   8 _ _ _ _ _

9 _ _ _ _   10 _ _ _

then I put it back again.

  cod     dabs

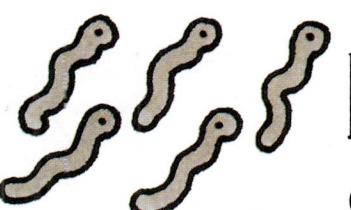  eels      crabs

Write the missing letters.

Colour the words on the big card to match the words on the small cards.

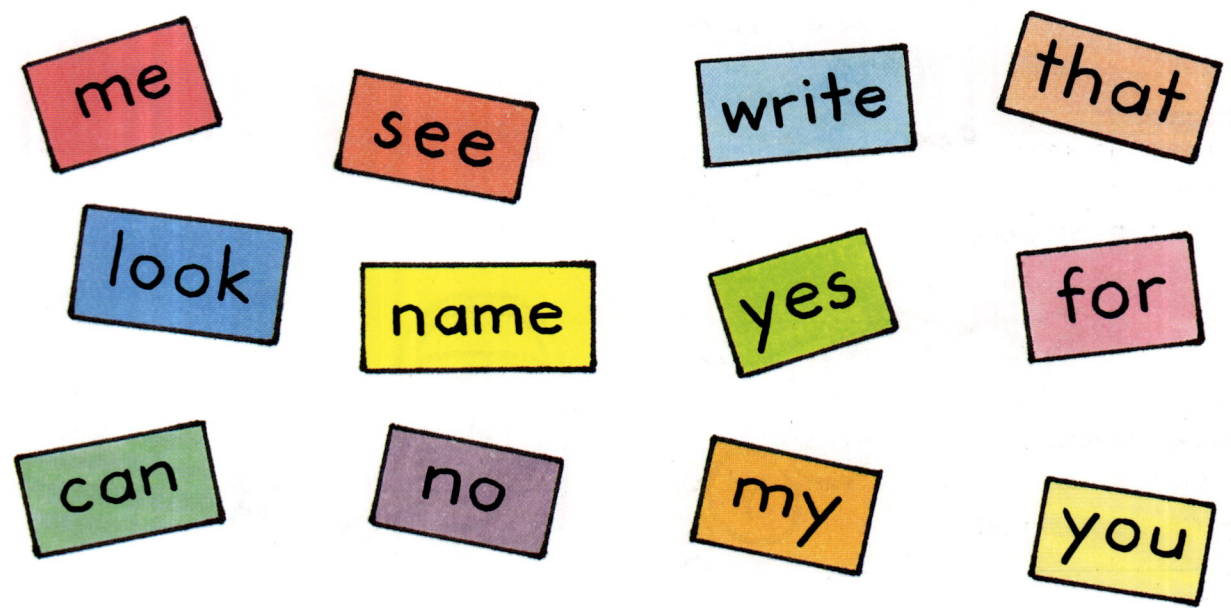